50 Chinese Takeout Favorites Made Healthy Recipes for Home

By: Kelly Johnson

Table of Contents

- General Tso's Chicken
- Beef and Broccoli Stir-Fry
- Sweet and Sour Pork
- Kung Pao Chicken
- Egg Fried Rice
- Shrimp Lo Mein
- Vegetable Spring Rolls
- Orange Chicken
- Sesame Chicken
- Moo Goo Gai Pan
- Cashew Chicken
- Garlic Beef Stir-Fry
- Chicken Chow Mein
- Honey Garlic Shrimp
- Lemon Chicken
- Szechuan Beef
- Teriyaki Chicken
- Vegetable Fried Rice
- Mongolian Beef
- Crab Rangoon
- Pepper Steak
- Chicken and Broccoli Stir-Fry
- Sweet and Spicy Tofu
- Shrimp and Snow Peas
- Singapore Noodles
- General Tso's Tofu
- Sesame Shrimp
- Moo Shu Pork
- Garlic Shrimp Fried Rice
- Chicken Lettuce Wraps
- Hunan Chicken
- Shrimp with Garlic Sauce
- Beef Chow Fun
- Five-Spice Pork Ribs
- Honey Walnut Shrimp

- Veggie Lo Mein
- Lemon Garlic Broccoli
- Pineapple Chicken
- Crispy Tofu with Chili Sauce
- Vegetable Chow Fun
- Sweet and Sour Tofu
- Spicy Szechuan Shrimp
- Hot and Sour Soup
- Chicken and Cashew Nuts
- General Tso's Cauliflower
- Shrimp and Lobster Sauce
- Beef with Oyster Sauce
- Veggie Spring Roll Bowls
- Sesame Ginger Bok Choy
- Crispy Orange Tofu

General Tso's Chicken

Ingredients:

- 1 lb boneless, skinless chicken breasts, cut into bite-sized pieces
- 1/2 cup cornstarch
- 2 tablespoons vegetable oil, for frying
- 3 cloves garlic, minced
- 1 tablespoon ginger, minced
- 1/2 cup low-sodium soy sauce
- 1/4 cup hoisin sauce
- 3 tablespoons rice vinegar
- 3 tablespoons brown sugar
- 1 teaspoon sesame oil
- 1/4 teaspoon red pepper flakes (optional)
- 2 green onions, sliced
- Cooked white rice, for serving
- Sesame seeds, for garnish (optional)

Instructions:

1. In a bowl, toss the chicken pieces with cornstarch until well coated.
2. Heat vegetable oil in a large skillet or wok over medium-high heat. Fry the chicken in batches until golden brown and cooked through, about 4-5 minutes per batch. Remove chicken and set aside.
3. In the same skillet, add a bit more oil if needed and sauté garlic and ginger until fragrant, about 1 minute.
4. Add soy sauce, hoisin sauce, rice vinegar, brown sugar, sesame oil, and red pepper flakes (if using). Stir until the sauce thickens slightly, about 2-3 minutes.
5. Return the cooked chicken to the skillet and toss to coat evenly with the sauce.
6. Serve General Tso's Chicken over cooked white rice, garnished with sliced green onions and sesame seeds if desired. Enjoy!

Note: Adjust the amount of red pepper flakes according to your desired level of spiciness. You can also add more vegetables such as broccoli or bell peppers to the dish for extra flavor and nutrition.

Beef and Broccoli Stir-Fry

Ingredients:

- 1 lb (450g) beef steak (flank steak or sirloin), sliced thinly against the grain
- 2 cups broccoli florets
- 2 tablespoons vegetable oil
- 3 cloves garlic, minced
- 1 tablespoon fresh ginger, minced
- 1/4 cup soy sauce
- 2 tablespoons oyster sauce
- 1 tablespoon brown sugar
- 1 tablespoon cornstarch
- 1/4 cup water
- Sesame seeds (optional, for garnish)
- Cooked rice or noodles, for serving

Instructions:

Marinate the Beef:
- In a bowl, combine soy sauce, oyster sauce, brown sugar, minced garlic, and minced ginger.
- Add the sliced beef to the marinade and let it marinate for at least 15-30 minutes in the refrigerator.

Prepare the Sauce:
- In a separate bowl, mix cornstarch with water until dissolved. This will help thicken the sauce later.

Stir-Fry the Broccoli:
- Heat 1 tablespoon of vegetable oil in a large skillet or wok over medium-high heat.
- Add the broccoli florets to the skillet and stir-fry for about 3-4 minutes until they are bright green and slightly tender. Remove them from the skillet and set aside.

Cook the Beef:
- In the same skillet, add another tablespoon of oil if needed.
- Add the marinated beef slices to the skillet and stir-fry for 2-3 minutes until they are browned and cooked through.

Combine Everything:

- Return the cooked broccoli to the skillet with the beef.
- Give the cornstarch mixture a quick stir and pour it into the skillet.
- Stir everything together and let it cook for another minute or until the sauce thickens and coats the beef and broccoli evenly.

Serve:
- Remove the skillet from heat.
- Sprinkle sesame seeds on top for garnish if desired.
- Serve the beef and broccoli stir-fry hot over cooked rice or noodles.

Enjoy your homemade beef and broccoli stir-fry! Feel free to adjust the seasoning or add other vegetables according to your preference.

Sweet and Sour Pork

Ingredients:

For the pork:

- 1 lb (450g) pork tenderloin or pork shoulder, cut into bite-sized pieces
- 1/2 cup cornstarch
- 2 eggs, beaten
- Salt and pepper to taste
- Vegetable oil for frying

For the sauce:

- 1/2 cup ketchup
- 1/4 cup rice vinegar or white vinegar
- 1/4 cup brown sugar
- 2 tablespoons soy sauce
- 1 tablespoon cornstarch
- 1/4 cup water

For the stir-fry:

- 1 bell pepper, cut into chunks
- 1 onion, cut into chunks
- 1 cup pineapple chunks (fresh or canned)
- 2 cloves garlic, minced
- 1 tablespoon ginger, minced
- Sliced green onions for garnish (optional)
- Cooked rice for serving

Instructions:

Prepare the Pork:
- In a bowl, season the pork pieces with salt and pepper.
- Coat the pork pieces with cornstarch, shaking off any excess.
- Dip each piece into the beaten eggs, coating evenly.

Fry the Pork:
- Heat vegetable oil in a large skillet or deep fryer to 350°F (175°C).
- Fry the pork pieces in batches until golden brown and cooked through, about 3-4 minutes per batch. Remove them from the oil and drain on paper towels.

Make the Sauce:
- In a small saucepan, combine ketchup, rice vinegar, brown sugar, and soy sauce.
- In a separate bowl, mix cornstarch with water until dissolved.
- Add the cornstarch mixture to the saucepan.
- Cook the sauce over medium heat, stirring constantly, until it thickens. Remove from heat.

Stir-Fry the Vegetables:
- In a separate large skillet or wok, heat a little oil over medium-high heat.
- Add minced garlic and ginger to the skillet and stir-fry for about 1 minute until fragrant.
- Add bell pepper, onion, and pineapple chunks to the skillet. Stir-fry for another 2-3 minutes until vegetables are tender-crisp.

Combine Everything:
- Add the fried pork pieces to the skillet with the vegetables.
- Pour the sweet and sour sauce over the pork and vegetables.
- Stir everything together until the pork and vegetables are coated evenly with the sauce.

Serve:
- Garnish with sliced green onions if desired.
- Serve the sweet and sour pork hot over cooked rice.

Enjoy your homemade sweet and sour pork! Adjust the sweetness or tanginess of the sauce according to your taste preference.

Kung Pao Chicken

Ingredients:

- 1 lb (450g) boneless, skinless chicken breasts or thighs, cut into bite-sized pieces
- 1 tablespoon soy sauce
- 1 tablespoon rice wine or dry sherry
- 1 tablespoon cornstarch
- 2 tablespoons vegetable oil
- 3-4 dried red chili peppers, chopped (adjust according to your spice preference)
- 1 teaspoon Sichuan peppercorns (optional)
- 3 cloves garlic, minced
- 1-inch piece of ginger, minced
- 1 bell pepper, diced
- 1/2 cup unsalted peanuts
- 2 green onions, chopped, for garnish

For the sauce:

- 2 tablespoons soy sauce
- 1 tablespoon rice vinegar
- 1 tablespoon hoisin sauce
- 1 teaspoon sesame oil
- 1 teaspoon sugar
- 1 teaspoon cornstarch dissolved in 2 tablespoons water

Instructions:

In a bowl, mix the soy sauce, rice wine or sherry, and cornstarch. Add the chicken pieces and toss to coat. Let marinate for about 15-20 minutes.
In a small bowl, mix together the ingredients for the sauce: soy sauce, rice vinegar, hoisin sauce, sesame oil, sugar, and cornstarch mixture. Set aside.
Heat the vegetable oil in a large skillet or wok over medium-high heat. Add the dried chili peppers and Sichuan peppercorns (if using) and stir-fry for about 30 seconds until fragrant.
Add the marinated chicken to the skillet and stir-fry until cooked through, about 5-7 minutes.

Add the minced garlic, ginger, and diced bell pepper to the skillet. Stir-fry for another 2-3 minutes until the vegetables are tender-crisp.

Pour the prepared sauce over the chicken and vegetables in the skillet. Stir well to combine and cook for another 1-2 minutes until the sauce thickens slightly.

Add the unsalted peanuts to the skillet and stir to combine.

Garnish with chopped green onions and serve hot with steamed rice.

Enjoy your homemade Kung Pao Chicken! Adjust the level of spiciness and other seasonings according to your taste preferences.

Egg Fried Rice

Ingredients:

- 3 cups cooked rice (preferably day-old rice)
- 2 eggs, beaten
- 1 cup mixed vegetables (such as peas, carrots, bell peppers, and onions)
- 2 cloves garlic, minced
- 2 tablespoons soy sauce
- 1 tablespoon oyster sauce (optional)
- 2 tablespoons vegetable oil
- Salt and pepper to taste
- Green onions or cilantro for garnish (optional)

Instructions:

Heat one tablespoon of vegetable oil in a large skillet or wok over medium-high heat.
Add the beaten eggs to the skillet and scramble them until they're cooked through. Remove them from the skillet and set aside.
In the same skillet, add the remaining tablespoon of vegetable oil. Add the minced garlic and cook for about 30 seconds until fragrant.
Add the mixed vegetables to the skillet and stir-fry for 2-3 minutes until they're slightly tender.
Add the cooked rice to the skillet, breaking up any clumps with a spatula.
Pour the soy sauce and oyster sauce (if using) over the rice and vegetables. Stir well to combine.
Add the cooked eggs back into the skillet and mix everything together until the eggs are evenly distributed.
Cook for another 2-3 minutes, stirring occasionally, until everything is heated through.
Season with salt and pepper to taste.
Garnish with chopped green onions or cilantro if desired.
Serve hot and enjoy your delicious egg fried rice!

Feel free to customize this recipe by adding your favorite protein (such as chicken, shrimp, or tofu) or adjusting the vegetables according to your preference.

Shrimp Lo Mein

Ingredients:

- 8 oz lo mein noodles or spaghetti
- 1/2 lb shrimp, peeled and deveined
- 2 cups mixed vegetables (such as bell peppers, carrots, broccoli, and snap peas), sliced
- 3 cloves garlic, minced
- 2 tablespoons vegetable oil
- 2 tablespoons soy sauce
- 1 tablespoon oyster sauce
- 1 tablespoon hoisin sauce
- 1 teaspoon sesame oil
- 1/2 teaspoon sugar
- Salt and pepper to taste
- Chopped green onions for garnish (optional)
- Sesame seeds for garnish (optional)

Instructions:

Cook the lo mein noodles according to the package instructions until they are al dente. Drain and set aside.
In a small bowl, mix together the soy sauce, oyster sauce, hoisin sauce, sesame oil, and sugar. Set aside.
Heat one tablespoon of vegetable oil in a large skillet or wok over medium-high heat.
Add the shrimp to the skillet and stir-fry for 2-3 minutes until they turn pink and opaque. Remove the shrimp from the skillet and set aside.
In the same skillet, add the remaining tablespoon of vegetable oil. Add the minced garlic and stir-fry for about 30 seconds until fragrant.
Add the mixed vegetables to the skillet and stir-fry for 3-4 minutes until they're tender-crisp.
Return the cooked shrimp to the skillet, along with the cooked lo mein noodles. Pour the sauce mixture over the shrimp, noodles, and vegetables. Stir well to combine and coat everything evenly with the sauce.
Cook for another 2-3 minutes, stirring occasionally, until everything is heated through.

Season with salt and pepper to taste.
Garnish with chopped green onions and sesame seeds if desired.
Serve hot and enjoy your delicious shrimp lo mein!

Feel free to customize this recipe by adding other ingredients like mushrooms, bok choy, or water chestnuts, according to your taste preferences.

Vegetable Spring Rolls

Ingredients:

For the filling:

- 2 cups shredded cabbage
- 1 cup shredded carrots
- 1 cup bean sprouts
- 1 bell pepper, thinly sliced
- 1 small onion, thinly sliced
- 2 cloves garlic, minced
- 1 tablespoon soy sauce
- 1 tablespoon sesame oil
- Salt and pepper to taste
- 2 tablespoons vegetable oil for stir-frying

For assembling:

- Spring roll wrappers (available at Asian grocery stores)
- 1 tablespoon cornstarch mixed with 2 tablespoons water (as a sealant)
- Vegetable oil for frying

Instructions:

Heat 2 tablespoons of vegetable oil in a large skillet or wok over medium-high heat.
Add the minced garlic and sliced onion to the skillet and stir-fry for about 1 minute until fragrant.
Add the shredded cabbage, carrots, bean sprouts, and bell pepper to the skillet. Stir-fry for 3-4 minutes until the vegetables are slightly softened but still crisp.
Season the vegetables with soy sauce, sesame oil, salt, and pepper. Stir well to combine. Remove the skillet from heat and let the filling cool down.

Assembling the spring rolls:

Lay a spring roll wrapper on a clean, flat surface. Place about 2 tablespoons of the vegetable filling in the center of the wrapper.

Fold the bottom edge of the wrapper over the filling, then fold in the sides, and roll tightly into a cylinder shape. Use the cornstarch-water mixture to seal the edges of the wrapper.

Repeat with the remaining wrappers and filling until all the filling is used up.

Cooking the spring rolls:

Heat vegetable oil in a deep fryer or a large skillet over medium heat. The oil should be hot but not smoking.

Carefully add the spring rolls to the hot oil, a few at a time, making sure not to overcrowd the pan.

Fry the spring rolls for 2-3 minutes on each side until they are golden brown and crispy.

Remove the spring rolls from the oil and drain them on paper towels to remove excess oil.

Serve the vegetable spring rolls hot with your favorite dipping sauce, such as sweet chili sauce, plum sauce, or soy sauce mixed with a splash of rice vinegar. Enjoy!

Orange Chicken

Ingredients:

For the chicken:

- 1 lb boneless, skinless chicken breasts or thighs, cut into bite-sized pieces
- 1 cup cornstarch
- 2 eggs, beaten
- Salt and pepper to taste
- Vegetable oil for frying

For the orange sauce:

- 1/2 cup orange juice
- Zest of 1 orange
- 1/4 cup soy sauce
- 3 tablespoons rice vinegar
- 3 tablespoons brown sugar
- 2 cloves garlic, minced
- 1 teaspoon fresh ginger, grated
- 1 tablespoon cornstarch mixed with 2 tablespoons water (as a thickener)
- Sesame seeds and sliced green onions for garnish (optional)

Instructions:

In a bowl, season the chicken pieces with salt and pepper.
Place the cornstarch in a separate bowl. Dip each chicken piece into the beaten eggs, then coat evenly with cornstarch, shaking off any excess.
Heat vegetable oil in a large skillet or deep fryer over medium-high heat. Fry the chicken pieces in batches for 5-6 minutes until golden brown and cooked through. Transfer the fried chicken to a plate lined with paper towels to drain excess oil.
In a saucepan, combine orange juice, orange zest, soy sauce, rice vinegar, brown sugar, minced garlic, and grated ginger. Bring the mixture to a simmer over medium heat.

Stir in the cornstarch-water mixture and continue to simmer, stirring constantly, until the sauce thickens and becomes glossy.

Add the fried chicken pieces to the sauce and toss to coat evenly.

Cook for an additional 2-3 minutes, allowing the chicken to absorb the flavors of the sauce.

Remove from heat and garnish with sesame seeds and sliced green onions, if desired.

Serve hot with steamed rice or noodles.

Enjoy your homemade orange chicken! Adjust the sweetness or tanginess of the sauce according to your taste preference by adjusting the amount of brown sugar or vinegar.

Sesame Chicken

Ingredients:

For the chicken:

- 1 lb boneless, skinless chicken breasts, cut into bite-sized pieces
- 1/2 cup cornstarch
- 2 eggs, beaten
- Salt and pepper to taste
- Vegetable oil for frying

For the sauce:

- 1/4 cup soy sauce
- 2 tablespoons hoisin sauce
- 2 tablespoons honey
- 2 cloves garlic, minced
- 1 tablespoon rice vinegar
- 1 tablespoon sesame oil
- 1 tablespoon cornstarch mixed with 2 tablespoons water (as a thickener)

For garnish:

- Sesame seeds
- Sliced green onions (optional)

Instructions:

In a bowl, season the chicken pieces with salt and pepper.
Place the cornstarch in a separate bowl. Dip each chicken piece into the beaten eggs, then coat evenly with cornstarch, shaking off any excess.
Heat vegetable oil in a large skillet or deep fryer over medium-high heat. Fry the chicken pieces in batches for 5-6 minutes until golden brown and cooked through. Transfer the fried chicken to a plate lined with paper towels to drain excess oil.

In a small saucepan, combine soy sauce, hoisin sauce, honey, minced garlic, rice vinegar, and sesame oil. Bring the mixture to a simmer over medium heat.

Stir in the cornstarch-water mixture and continue to simmer, stirring constantly, until the sauce thickens and becomes glossy.

Add the fried chicken pieces to the sauce and toss to coat evenly.

Cook for an additional 2-3 minutes, allowing the chicken to absorb the flavors of the sauce.

Remove from heat and garnish with sesame seeds and sliced green onions, if desired.

Serve hot with steamed rice or noodles.

Enjoy your homemade sesame chicken! Adjust the sweetness or saltiness of the sauce according to your taste preference by adjusting the amount of honey or soy sauce.

Moo Goo Gai Pan

Ingredients:

For the chicken marinade:

- 1 lb boneless, skinless chicken breasts, thinly sliced
- 2 tablespoons soy sauce
- 1 tablespoon rice wine or dry sherry
- 1 teaspoon cornstarch

For the sauce:

- 1/2 cup chicken broth
- 2 tablespoons oyster sauce
- 1 tablespoon soy sauce
- 1 tablespoon rice wine or dry sherry
- 1 teaspoon cornstarch

For the stir-fry:

- 2 tablespoons vegetable oil
- 2 cloves garlic, minced
- 1 teaspoon fresh ginger, grated
- 8 oz mushrooms (such as button or shiitake), sliced
- 1 cup snow peas, trimmed
- 1 cup sliced carrots
- 1 cup sliced bell peppers (any color)
- 1 cup sliced bamboo shoots (optional)
- Salt and pepper to taste
- Sliced green onions for garnish (optional)
- Cooked rice for serving

Instructions:

In a bowl, combine the sliced chicken with soy sauce, rice wine or sherry, and cornstarch. Mix well and let it marinate for at least 15 minutes.

In another bowl, whisk together the chicken broth, oyster sauce, soy sauce, rice wine or sherry, and cornstarch to make the sauce. Set aside.

Heat 1 tablespoon of vegetable oil in a large skillet or wok over medium-high heat. Add the marinated chicken slices and stir-fry for 3-4 minutes until they are no longer pink. Remove the chicken from the skillet and set aside.

In the same skillet, add another tablespoon of vegetable oil. Add the minced garlic and grated ginger, and stir-fry for about 30 seconds until fragrant.

Add the sliced mushrooms to the skillet and cook for 2-3 minutes until they start to soften.

Add the snow peas, sliced carrots, bell peppers, and bamboo shoots (if using) to the skillet. Stir-fry for another 2-3 minutes until the vegetables are tender-crisp.

Return the cooked chicken to the skillet and pour the sauce over the chicken and vegetables. Stir well to coat everything evenly with the sauce.

Cook for an additional 2-3 minutes, stirring constantly, until the sauce thickens and everything is heated through.

Season with salt and pepper to taste.

Garnish with sliced green onions if desired.

Serve hot with cooked rice.

Enjoy your homemade Moo Goo Gai Pan! Feel free to adjust the vegetables according to your preference or what you have on hand.

Cashew Chicken

Ingredients:

For the chicken marinade:

- 1 lb boneless, skinless chicken breasts, cut into bite-sized pieces
- 2 tablespoons soy sauce
- 1 tablespoon rice wine or dry sherry
- 1 teaspoon cornstarch

For the sauce:

- 1/4 cup chicken broth
- 2 tablespoons soy sauce
- 1 tablespoon oyster sauce
- 1 tablespoon hoisin sauce
- 1 teaspoon rice vinegar
- 1 teaspoon sesame oil
- 1 teaspoon cornstarch

For the stir-fry:

- 2 tablespoons vegetable oil
- 2 cloves garlic, minced
- 1 teaspoon fresh ginger, grated
- 1 bell pepper, diced
- 1 cup broccoli florets
- 1/2 cup sliced carrots
- 1/2 cup unsalted cashews
- Salt and pepper to taste
- Sliced green onions for garnish (optional)
- Cooked rice for serving

Instructions:

In a bowl, combine the chicken pieces with soy sauce, rice wine or sherry, and cornstarch. Mix well and let it marinate for at least 15 minutes.

In another bowl, whisk together the chicken broth, soy sauce, oyster sauce, hoisin sauce, rice vinegar, sesame oil, and cornstarch to make the sauce. Set aside.

Heat 1 tablespoon of vegetable oil in a large skillet or wok over medium-high heat. Add the marinated chicken pieces and stir-fry for 3-4 minutes until they are no longer pink. Remove the chicken from the skillet and set aside.

In the same skillet, add another tablespoon of vegetable oil. Add the minced garlic and grated ginger, and stir-fry for about 30 seconds until fragrant.

Add the diced bell pepper, broccoli florets, and sliced carrots to the skillet. Stir-fry for 2-3 minutes until the vegetables are tender-crisp.

Return the cooked chicken to the skillet and pour the sauce over the chicken and vegetables. Stir well to coat everything evenly with the sauce.

Cook for an additional 2-3 minutes, stirring constantly, until the sauce thickens and everything is heated through.

Stir in the cashews and cook for another minute until they are warmed through.

Season with salt and pepper to taste.

Garnish with sliced green onions if desired.

Serve hot with cooked rice.

Enjoy your homemade cashew chicken! Adjust the seasoning or add more vegetables according to your taste preferences.

Garlic Beef Stir-Fry

Ingredients:

For the marinade:

- 1 lb beef sirloin, thinly sliced
- 2 tablespoons soy sauce
- 1 tablespoon oyster sauce
- 1 tablespoon cornstarch
- 1 teaspoon sesame oil
- 2 cloves garlic, minced
- 1 teaspoon ginger, minced

For the stir-fry:

- 2 tablespoons vegetable oil
- 4 cloves garlic, minced
- 1 onion, sliced
- 1 bell pepper, sliced
- 1 cup broccoli florets
- 1 cup snap peas or snow peas
- Salt and pepper to taste
- Sesame seeds for garnish (optional)
- Sliced green onions for garnish (optional)

For the sauce:

- 3 tablespoons soy sauce
- 2 tablespoons oyster sauce
- 1 tablespoon hoisin sauce
- 1 tablespoon rice vinegar
- 1 tablespoon brown sugar
- 1 teaspoon sesame oil
- 1 teaspoon cornstarch dissolved in 2 tablespoons water

Instructions:

In a bowl, combine the thinly sliced beef with soy sauce, oyster sauce, cornstarch, sesame oil, minced garlic, and minced ginger. Mix well to ensure the beef is evenly coated. Let it marinate for at least 15-20 minutes.

In another bowl, prepare the sauce by combining soy sauce, oyster sauce, hoisin sauce, rice vinegar, brown sugar, and sesame oil. Stir well to combine. Dissolve cornstarch in water and add it to the sauce, stirring until well incorporated. Set aside.

Heat 1 tablespoon of vegetable oil in a large skillet or wok over high heat. Once hot, add the marinated beef slices and stir-fry for 2-3 minutes until browned and cooked through. Remove the beef from the skillet and set aside.

In the same skillet, heat the remaining tablespoon of vegetable oil. Add minced garlic and sauté for about 30 seconds until fragrant.

Add sliced onion, bell pepper, broccoli florets, and snap peas to the skillet. Stir-fry for 3-4 minutes until the vegetables are tender-crisp.

Return the cooked beef to the skillet. Pour the sauce over the beef and vegetables, stirring to coat everything evenly. Cook for another 1-2 minutes until the sauce thickens.

Season with salt and pepper to taste.

Garnish with sesame seeds and sliced green onions if desired.

Serve hot with steamed rice or noodles.

Enjoy your flavorful Garlic Beef Stir-Fry! Feel free to adjust the vegetables according to your preference or what you have on hand.

Chicken Chow Mein

Ingredients:

- 250g egg noodles
- 2 chicken breasts, thinly sliced
- 2 tablespoons vegetable oil
- 2 garlic cloves, minced
- 1 onion, sliced
- 1 carrot, julienned
- 1 bell pepper, sliced
- 1 cup cabbage, shredded
- 2 spring onions, chopped
- 2 tablespoons soy sauce
- 1 tablespoon oyster sauce
- 1 teaspoon sesame oil
- Salt and pepper to taste

Instructions:

Cook the egg noodles according to the package instructions. Drain and set aside. Heat 1 tablespoon of vegetable oil in a large skillet or wok over medium-high heat. Add the sliced chicken breasts and cook until they are browned and cooked through. Remove the chicken from the skillet and set aside.

In the same skillet, heat the remaining tablespoon of vegetable oil. Add the minced garlic and sliced onion, and stir-fry for about 1-2 minutes until fragrant. Add the julienned carrot, sliced bell pepper, and shredded cabbage to the skillet. Stir-fry for another 3-4 minutes until the vegetables are tender-crisp.

Return the cooked chicken to the skillet. Add the cooked egg noodles and toss everything together.

In a small bowl, mix together the soy sauce, oyster sauce, and sesame oil. Pour the sauce over the noodles and chicken mixture. Stir well to combine and coat everything evenly. Season with salt and pepper to taste.

Continue to stir-fry for another 2-3 minutes until everything is heated through and well combined.

Garnish the Chicken Chow Mein with chopped spring onions before serving.

Enjoy your homemade Chicken Chow Mein!

Honey Garlic Shrimp

Ingredients:

- 1 pound large shrimp, peeled and deveined
- 3 cloves garlic, minced
- 2 tablespoons honey
- 2 tablespoons soy sauce
- 1 tablespoon olive oil
- 1 tablespoon butter
- Salt and pepper to taste
- Chopped green onions for garnish (optional)
- Sesame seeds for garnish (optional)

Instructions:

Marinate the shrimp: In a bowl, mix together the minced garlic, honey, and soy sauce. Add the shrimp to the bowl and toss to coat evenly. Allow the shrimp to marinate for at least 15-20 minutes in the refrigerator.

Cook the shrimp: Heat olive oil and butter in a large skillet over medium-high heat. Once the skillet is hot, add the marinated shrimp in a single layer. Cook for 2-3 minutes on each side, or until the shrimp turn pink and opaque. Be careful not to overcook the shrimp, as they can become tough.

Add the sauce: After the shrimp are cooked, pour any remaining marinade into the skillet. Allow the sauce to come to a simmer and cook for an additional minute, stirring occasionally, until it thickens slightly and coats the shrimp. Season with salt and pepper to taste.

Garnish and serve: Once the sauce has thickened, remove the skillet from the heat. Garnish the shrimp with chopped green onions and sesame seeds if desired. Serve the honey garlic shrimp hot, either on its own or with rice or noodles as a side dish.

Enjoy your delicious honey garlic shrimp!

Lemon Chicken

Ingredients:

- 4 boneless, skinless chicken breasts
- Salt and pepper to taste
- 1/2 cup all-purpose flour
- 2 tablespoons olive oil
- 2 tablespoons butter
- 4 cloves garlic, minced
- 1 cup chicken broth
- 1/4 cup freshly squeezed lemon juice (about 2 lemons)
- Zest of 1 lemon
- 2 tablespoons capers, drained (optional)
- 2 tablespoons chopped fresh parsley for garnish

Instructions:

Prepare the chicken: Season the chicken breasts with salt and pepper on both sides. Dredge each chicken breast in flour, shaking off any excess.
Cook the chicken: Heat olive oil and butter in a large skillet over medium-high heat. Once the skillet is hot, add the chicken breasts in a single layer. Cook for 4-5 minutes on each side, or until golden brown and cooked through. Remove the chicken from the skillet and set aside.
Make the lemon sauce: In the same skillet, add minced garlic and cook for about 1 minute until fragrant. Be careful not to burn the garlic. Pour in the chicken broth, lemon juice, and lemon zest. Bring the mixture to a simmer and cook for 2-3 minutes, stirring occasionally, until slightly reduced.
Add the chicken back: Return the cooked chicken breasts to the skillet, along with any juices that may have accumulated. Add capers if using. Spoon the lemon sauce over the chicken and let it simmer for another 2-3 minutes to allow the flavors to meld together.
Garnish and serve: Once the chicken is heated through and the sauce has thickened slightly, remove the skillet from the heat. Garnish the lemon chicken with chopped parsley. Serve hot, with additional lemon slices if desired.

Enjoy your delicious lemon chicken! It's perfect for a light and refreshing meal.

Szechuan Beef

Ingredients:

- 1 pound beef sirloin, thinly sliced against the grain
- 2 tablespoons soy sauce
- 1 tablespoon Shaoxing wine or dry sherry
- 1 tablespoon cornstarch
- 2 tablespoons vegetable oil, divided
- 4 cloves garlic, minced
- 1 tablespoon ginger, minced
- 2-3 dried red chilies, chopped (adjust to taste)
- 1/2 teaspoon Szechuan peppercorns, crushed
- 1 bell pepper, sliced
- 1 small onion, sliced
- 2 green onions, sliced (for garnish)
- Cooked rice, for serving

For the sauce:

- 2 tablespoons soy sauce
- 1 tablespoon hoisin sauce
- 1 tablespoon rice vinegar
- 1 tablespoon brown sugar
- 1 teaspoon sesame oil
- 1 teaspoon cornstarch mixed with 2 tablespoons water

Instructions:

Marinate the beef: In a bowl, combine thinly sliced beef with soy sauce, Shaoxing wine (or dry sherry), and cornstarch. Mix well and let it marinate for at least 15-20 minutes.
Prepare the sauce: In another bowl, whisk together soy sauce, hoisin sauce, rice vinegar, brown sugar, sesame oil, and the cornstarch-water mixture. Set aside.
Cook the beef: Heat 1 tablespoon of vegetable oil in a large skillet or wok over high heat. Once hot, add the marinated beef slices in a single layer and cook for 2-3 minutes until browned. Remove the beef from the skillet and set aside.
Stir-fry aromatics: In the same skillet, add another tablespoon of vegetable oil if needed. Add minced garlic, minced ginger, dried red chilies, and crushed Szechuan peppercorns. Stir-fry for about 30 seconds until fragrant.

Add vegetables: Add sliced bell pepper and onion to the skillet. Stir-fry for 2-3 minutes until they begin to soften.

Combine everything: Return the cooked beef to the skillet. Pour the prepared sauce over the beef and vegetables. Stir well to coat everything evenly.

Finish and serve: Cook for an additional 1-2 minutes until the sauce thickens and coats the beef and vegetables. Garnish with sliced green onions.

Serve: Serve the Szechuan beef hot over cooked rice.

Enjoy your homemade Szechuan beef! Adjust the amount of dried red chilies according to your desired level of spiciness.

Teriyaki Chicken

Ingredients:

- 4 boneless, skinless chicken thighs or breasts
- Salt and pepper to taste
- 1 tablespoon vegetable oil
- Sesame seeds and sliced green onions for garnish (optional)

For the teriyaki sauce:

- 1/4 cup soy sauce
- 1/4 cup mirin (Japanese sweet rice wine)
- 2 tablespoons sake or dry white wine (optional)
- 2 tablespoons honey or brown sugar
- 2 cloves garlic, minced
- 1 teaspoon grated ginger
- 1 teaspoon cornstarch mixed with 1 tablespoon water

Instructions:

Prepare the chicken: Season the chicken thighs or breasts with salt and pepper on both sides.

Make the teriyaki sauce: In a small saucepan, combine soy sauce, mirin, sake (if using), honey or brown sugar, minced garlic, and grated ginger. Heat the mixture over medium heat, stirring occasionally, until the sugar is dissolved and the sauce begins to simmer.

Thicken the sauce: In a small bowl, mix cornstarch with water to create a slurry. Add the slurry to the simmering sauce and whisk continuously until the sauce thickens slightly. Remove the sauce from heat and set aside.

Cook the chicken: Heat vegetable oil in a large skillet or grill pan over medium-high heat. Once hot, add the chicken pieces in a single layer. Cook for about 5-6 minutes on each side, or until the chicken is cooked through and nicely browned.

Glaze the chicken: Pour the prepared teriyaki sauce over the cooked chicken in the skillet. Let it simmer for 1-2 minutes, flipping the chicken occasionally to coat it evenly with the sauce.

Garnish and serve: Once the chicken is glazed and cooked through, remove it from the skillet. Garnish with sesame seeds and sliced green onions if desired.

Serve: Serve the teriyaki chicken hot, either on its own or with steamed rice and vegetables.

Enjoy your homemade teriyaki chicken! Adjust the sweetness or saltiness of the sauce according to your taste preferences.

Vegetable Fried Rice

Ingredients:

- 3 cups cooked rice (preferably day-old rice)
- 2 tablespoons vegetable oil
- 2 cloves garlic, minced
- 1 small onion, finely chopped
- 2 carrots, diced
- 1 bell pepper, diced
- 1 cup frozen peas and carrots, thawed
- 2 eggs, lightly beaten
- 3 tablespoons soy sauce
- 1 tablespoon oyster sauce (optional)
- Salt and pepper to taste
- 2 green onions, thinly sliced (for garnish)
- Sesame seeds (optional, for garnish)

Instructions:

Prep the rice: If you're using freshly cooked rice, spread it out on a baking sheet to cool and dry out slightly. Day-old rice works best for fried rice as it's less sticky.
Cook the vegetables: Heat 1 tablespoon of vegetable oil in a large skillet or wok over medium-high heat. Add minced garlic and chopped onion, and sauté for 1-2 minutes until fragrant. Add diced carrots and cook for another 2-3 minutes until they start to soften. Then add diced bell pepper and frozen peas and carrots. Stir-fry for an additional 2-3 minutes until the vegetables are tender-crisp. Transfer the cooked vegetables to a plate and set aside.
Scramble the eggs: In the same skillet, add the remaining tablespoon of vegetable oil. Pour the lightly beaten eggs into the skillet and cook, stirring constantly, until they are scrambled and cooked through.
Combine everything: Return the cooked vegetables to the skillet with the scrambled eggs. Add the cooked rice to the skillet, breaking up any clumps with a spatula. Stir-fry everything together, mixing well to combine.
Add sauces: Drizzle soy sauce and oyster sauce (if using) over the rice mixture. Stir well to evenly distribute the sauces. Season with salt and pepper to taste.
Finish and garnish: Continue to stir-fry the rice mixture for another 2-3 minutes until everything is heated through and well combined. Taste and adjust seasoning if needed. Remove the skillet from heat.

Garnish and serve: Garnish the vegetable fried rice with thinly sliced green onions and sesame seeds if desired. Serve hot as a main dish or as a side dish with your favorite Asian-inspired meal.

Enjoy your homemade vegetable fried rice! Feel free to customize the recipe by adding other vegetables or proteins such as tofu, shrimp, or chicken.

Mongolian Beef

Ingredients:

- 1 pound flank steak or sirloin, sliced thinly against the grain
- 3 tablespoons cornstarch
- 1/4 cup vegetable oil (for frying)
- 2 cloves garlic, minced
- 1 teaspoon ginger, minced
- 1/2 cup low-sodium soy sauce
- 1/2 cup water
- 1/2 cup brown sugar
- 2 green onions, sliced diagonally for garnish
- Sesame seeds for garnish (optional)

Instructions:

Prepare the beef: In a bowl, toss the thinly sliced beef with cornstarch until evenly coated. This will help to tenderize the beef and thicken the sauce later.

Make the sauce: In another bowl, whisk together minced garlic, minced ginger, soy sauce, water, and brown sugar until the sugar is dissolved. Set the sauce aside.

Cook the beef: Heat vegetable oil in a large skillet or wok over high heat. Once the oil is hot, add the coated beef slices in a single layer, making sure not to overcrowd the pan. Cook for 1-2 minutes per side until browned and crispy. You may need to do this in batches. Remove the cooked beef from the skillet and set aside.

Make the dish: In the same skillet, reduce the heat to medium. Add a little more oil if needed, then add the minced garlic and ginger. Stir-fry for about 30 seconds until fragrant.

Add the sauce: Pour the prepared sauce into the skillet with the garlic and ginger. Bring the sauce to a simmer and cook for 2-3 minutes until it starts to thicken slightly.

Combine everything: Return the cooked beef to the skillet, tossing it with the sauce until well coated. Cook for an additional 1-2 minutes until the beef is heated through and the sauce has thickened to your desired consistency.

Garnish and serve: Garnish the Mongolian beef with sliced green onions and sesame seeds if desired. Serve hot over steamed rice or noodles.

Enjoy your homemade Mongolian beef! Adjust the sweetness or saltiness of the sauce according to your taste preferences.

Crab Rangoon

Ingredients:

- 8 oz (225g) cream cheese, softened
- 1 cup crab meat (canned or imitation), chopped
- 2 green onions, finely chopped
- 1 clove garlic, minced
- 1 teaspoon Worcestershire sauce
- 1/2 teaspoon soy sauce
- 1/4 teaspoon garlic powder
- 1/4 teaspoon onion powder
- 1/4 teaspoon ground black pepper
- 24 wonton wrappers
- Vegetable oil for frying
- Sweet and sour sauce or sweet chili sauce for dipping (optional)

Instructions:

Prepare the filling: In a mixing bowl, combine softened cream cheese, chopped crab meat, finely chopped green onions, minced garlic, Worcestershire sauce, soy sauce, garlic powder, onion powder, and black pepper. Mix well until all ingredients are evenly incorporated.

Assemble the Crab Rangoon: Place about 1 tablespoon of the filling in the center of each wonton wrapper. Moisten the edges of the wrapper with water using your finger. Fold the wrapper diagonally to form a triangle, pressing the edges firmly to seal. You can also fold the wrapper into a traditional pouch shape if preferred.

Heat the oil: In a deep skillet or pot, heat vegetable oil to 350°F (175°C) over medium-high heat. You'll need enough oil to submerge the Crab Rangoon completely.

Fry the Crab Rangoon: Carefully add a few Crab Rangoon at a time to the hot oil, being careful not to overcrowd the pan. Fry for 2-3 minutes, turning occasionally, until golden brown and crispy. Use a slotted spoon to remove the fried Crab Rangoon from the oil and transfer them to a plate lined with paper towels to drain excess oil. Repeat until all Crab Rangoon are fried.

Serve: Serve the hot and crispy Crab Rangoon with sweet and sour sauce or sweet chili sauce for dipping.

Enjoy your homemade Crab Rangoon as a delicious appetizer for your next gathering or as a tasty snack!

Pepper Steak

Ingredients:

- 1 pound flank steak or sirloin, thinly sliced against the grain
- 2 tablespoons soy sauce
- 1 tablespoon cornstarch
- 2 tablespoons vegetable oil, divided
- 2 bell peppers (any color), sliced
- 1 onion, sliced
- 3 cloves garlic, minced
- 1 teaspoon ginger, minced
- 1/2 cup beef broth or water
- 2 tablespoons oyster sauce
- 1 tablespoon soy sauce
- 1 tablespoon cornstarch mixed with 2 tablespoons water (for thickening)
- Salt and pepper to taste
- Cooked rice for serving
- Sliced green onions and sesame seeds for garnish (optional)

Instructions:

Marinate the beef: In a bowl, combine thinly sliced beef with soy sauce and cornstarch. Mix well to coat the beef evenly. Let it marinate for at least 15-20 minutes.

Heat a skillet: Heat 1 tablespoon of vegetable oil in a large skillet or wok over high heat. Once the oil is hot, add the marinated beef slices in a single layer. Cook for 2-3 minutes until browned on one side, then flip and cook for another 2-3 minutes until browned and cooked through. Remove the beef from the skillet and set aside.

Cook the vegetables: In the same skillet, add another tablespoon of vegetable oil if needed. Add sliced bell peppers and onion to the skillet. Stir-fry for 2-3 minutes until the vegetables start to soften.

Make the sauce: Push the vegetables to one side of the skillet and add minced garlic and minced ginger to the empty space. Stir-fry for about 30 seconds until fragrant. Then, combine the vegetables with the garlic and ginger. Pour in beef broth (or water), oyster sauce, and soy sauce. Bring the mixture to a simmer.

Thicken the sauce: In a small bowl, mix cornstarch with water to create a slurry. Pour the slurry into the skillet, stirring continuously. Cook for 1-2 minutes until the sauce thickens to your desired consistency.

Add the beef back: Return the cooked beef slices to the skillet, tossing them with the sauce and vegetables until everything is evenly coated. Cook for an additional minute to heat through.

Serve: Serve the pepper steak hot over cooked rice. Garnish with sliced green onions and sesame seeds if desired.

Enjoy your homemade pepper steak! Adjust the seasoning and spice level according to your taste preferences.

Chicken and Broccoli Stir-Fry

Ingredients:

- 1 pound boneless, skinless chicken breasts or thighs, thinly sliced
- 2 tablespoons soy sauce
- 1 tablespoon oyster sauce
- 1 tablespoon cornstarch
- 1 tablespoon vegetable oil
- 2 cloves garlic, minced
- 1 teaspoon ginger, minced
- 1 head broccoli, cut into florets
- 1/2 cup chicken broth or water
- Salt and pepper to taste
- Cooked rice or noodles for serving
- Sesame seeds and sliced green onions for garnish (optional)

Instructions:

Marinate the chicken: In a bowl, combine thinly sliced chicken with soy sauce, oyster sauce, and cornstarch. Mix well to coat the chicken evenly. Let it marinate for about 15-20 minutes.

Heat a skillet: Heat vegetable oil in a large skillet or wok over medium-high heat. Once the oil is hot, add minced garlic and minced ginger. Stir-fry for about 30 seconds until fragrant.

Cook the chicken: Add the marinated chicken to the skillet in a single layer. Cook for 3-4 minutes, stirring occasionally, until the chicken is browned and cooked through. Remove the cooked chicken from the skillet and set aside.

Cook the broccoli: In the same skillet, add broccoli florets and chicken broth (or water). Cover and cook for 3-4 minutes until the broccoli is tender-crisp. If you prefer softer broccoli, cook for an additional 1-2 minutes.

Combine everything: Return the cooked chicken to the skillet with the broccoli. Stir everything together until well combined. Season with salt and pepper to taste.

Finish and serve: Cook for an additional minute to heat through. Serve the chicken and broccoli stir-fry hot over cooked rice or noodles.

Garnish and serve: Garnish with sesame seeds and sliced green onions if desired.

Enjoy your homemade chicken and broccoli stir-fry! It's a flavorful and wholesome meal that's perfect for busy weeknights. Feel free to customize the recipe by adding other vegetables like bell peppers, carrots, or snap peas.

Sweet and Spicy Tofu

Ingredients:

- 1 block of firm tofu, pressed and drained
- 2 tablespoons soy sauce
- 2 tablespoons honey or maple syrup
- 1 tablespoon sriracha sauce (adjust to taste)
- 1 tablespoon rice vinegar
- 1 tablespoon sesame oil
- 2 cloves garlic, minced
- 1 teaspoon grated ginger
- 1 tablespoon cornstarch
- 2 tablespoons water
- 2 green onions, chopped (optional)
- Sesame seeds for garnish (optional)
- Cooking oil for frying

Instructions:

Start by pressing the tofu to remove excess water. Place the block of tofu between two clean kitchen towels or paper towels, then place a heavy object on top (such as a plate or a pan). Let it sit for about 20-30 minutes.

While the tofu is being pressed, prepare the sauce. In a small bowl, mix together soy sauce, honey or maple syrup, sriracha sauce, rice vinegar, sesame oil, minced garlic, and grated ginger. Adjust the sweetness and spiciness according to your taste preference.

Once the tofu is pressed, cut it into cubes or slices, depending on your preference.

In a small bowl, mix cornstarch and water to create a slurry.

Heat cooking oil in a large skillet or non-stick pan over medium-high heat.

Dip each tofu piece into the cornstarch slurry, ensuring it's evenly coated.

Fry the tofu in the hot oil until golden brown and crispy on all sides, about 2-3 minutes per side. You may need to do this in batches depending on the size of your pan.

Once the tofu is crispy, remove it from the pan and place it on a plate lined with paper towels to absorb excess oil.

In the same skillet or pan, pour the prepared sauce mixture and let it simmer for a minute until slightly thickened.

Add the fried tofu back into the skillet and gently toss to coat each piece with the sauce. Cook for an additional minute, allowing the tofu to absorb the flavors of the sauce.

Garnish with chopped green onions and sesame seeds if desired.

Serve the sweet and spicy tofu hot with rice or your favorite side dishes. Enjoy your delicious meal!

Shrimp and Snow Peas

Ingredients:

- 1 lb (450g) large shrimp, peeled and deveined
- 1 cup snow peas, trimmed
- 1 red bell pepper, thinly sliced
- 3 cloves garlic, minced
- 1 tablespoon ginger, minced
- 2 tablespoons soy sauce
- 1 tablespoon oyster sauce
- 1 tablespoon rice vinegar
- 1 teaspoon sesame oil
- 1 teaspoon cornstarch
- 2 tablespoons water
- 2 tablespoons cooking oil (such as vegetable or peanut oil)
- Salt and pepper to taste
- Cooked rice for serving

Instructions:

In a small bowl, mix together soy sauce, oyster sauce, rice vinegar, sesame oil, cornstarch, and water to make the sauce. Set aside.

Heat 1 tablespoon of cooking oil in a large skillet or wok over medium-high heat.

Add the shrimp to the skillet and season with salt and pepper. Stir-fry the shrimp until they turn pink and opaque, about 2-3 minutes. Remove the shrimp from the skillet and set aside.

In the same skillet, add the remaining tablespoon of cooking oil.

Add minced garlic and ginger to the skillet and stir-fry for about 30 seconds until fragrant.

Add the sliced bell pepper and snow peas to the skillet. Stir-fry for 2-3 minutes until the vegetables are crisp-tender.

Return the cooked shrimp to the skillet.

Pour the sauce over the shrimp and vegetables. Stir well to coat everything evenly with the sauce.

Cook for an additional 1-2 minutes, stirring constantly, until the sauce thickens slightly and coats the shrimp and vegetables.

Taste and adjust seasoning with salt and pepper if necessary.

Remove from heat and serve the shrimp and snow peas stir-fry hot over cooked rice.
Garnish with chopped green onions or sesame seeds if desired.

Enjoy your delicious shrimp and snow peas stir-fry!

Singapore Noodles

Ingredients:

- 8 oz (225g) rice vermicelli noodles
- 1 tablespoon curry powder
- 2 tablespoons soy sauce
- 2 tablespoons vegetable oil
- 2 cloves garlic, minced
- 1 small onion, thinly sliced
- 1 red bell pepper, julienned
- 1 carrot, julienned
- 1 cup shredded cabbage
- 1 cup bean sprouts
- 1 cup cooked shrimp, chicken, or tofu (optional)
- 2 green onions, chopped
- Salt and pepper to taste
- Lime wedges for serving (optional)
- Fresh cilantro for garnish (optional)

Instructions:

Cook the rice vermicelli noodles according to the package instructions. Once cooked, drain and rinse the noodles under cold water to stop the cooking process. Set aside.

In a small bowl, mix together curry powder and soy sauce to create a paste. Set aside.

Heat vegetable oil in a large skillet or wok over medium-high heat.

Add minced garlic and sliced onion to the skillet. Stir-fry for about 1 minute until fragrant and the onion starts to soften.

Add julienned red bell pepper and carrot to the skillet. Stir-fry for another 2-3 minutes until the vegetables are slightly tender but still crisp.

Add shredded cabbage and bean sprouts to the skillet. Stir-fry for an additional 1-2 minutes until the cabbage begins to wilt.

Push the vegetables to one side of the skillet and add the curry paste to the empty space. Cook for about 30 seconds to 1 minute until fragrant.

Add the cooked rice vermicelli noodles to the skillet, along with the cooked shrimp, chicken, or tofu if using. Stir well to combine everything.

Pour the soy sauce over the noodles and vegetables. Stir-fry for another 2-3 minutes until everything is heated through and well coated with the sauce.
Taste and adjust seasoning with salt and pepper if necessary.
Remove from heat and garnish with chopped green onions and fresh cilantro if desired.
Serve the Singapore Noodles hot, optionally with lime wedges on the side for squeezing over the noodles.

Enjoy your delicious Singapore Noodles!

General Tso's Tofu

Ingredients:

- 1 block of firm tofu, pressed and cut into cubes
- 1/2 cup cornstarch
- 1/4 cup vegetable oil, for frying
- 2 tablespoons sesame oil
- 3 cloves garlic, minced
- 1 tablespoon fresh ginger, minced
- 1/2 cup soy sauce
- 1/2 cup water
- 1/4 cup hoisin sauce
- 2 tablespoons rice vinegar
- 2 tablespoons brown sugar
- 1 tablespoon cornstarch mixed with 2 tablespoons water (slurry)
- 2 green onions, chopped (for garnish)
- Cooked rice, for serving

Instructions:

Press the tofu to remove excess water. Cut it into cubes and toss the cubes in cornstarch until coated evenly.

Heat vegetable oil in a large skillet or wok over medium-high heat. Once the oil is hot, add the tofu cubes in batches and fry until golden brown and crispy. Remove the tofu cubes from the oil and place them on a paper towel-lined plate to drain excess oil.

In the same skillet, add sesame oil, minced garlic, and minced ginger. Stir-fry for about 30 seconds until fragrant.

In a bowl, mix together soy sauce, water, hoisin sauce, rice vinegar, and brown sugar. Pour this mixture into the skillet with garlic and ginger. Stir well to combine and bring to a simmer.

Once the sauce is simmering, add the cornstarch slurry to the skillet. Stir constantly until the sauce thickens.

Add the fried tofu cubes to the skillet and toss them gently to coat with the sauce.

Cook for another 2-3 minutes until the tofu is heated through and the sauce is thickened.

Remove from heat and garnish with chopped green onions.

Serve General Tso's Tofu hot over cooked rice.

Enjoy your homemade General Tso's Tofu!

Sesame Shrimp

Ingredients:

- 1 lb (450g) large shrimp, peeled and deveined
- 2 tablespoons soy sauce
- 1 tablespoon honey
- 1 tablespoon rice vinegar
- 1 tablespoon sesame oil
- 2 cloves garlic, minced
- 1 teaspoon grated ginger
- 2 tablespoons sesame seeds
- 2 green onions, thinly sliced (for garnish)
- Cooking oil (such as vegetable or peanut oil), for cooking
- Salt and pepper to taste

Instructions:

In a bowl, mix together soy sauce, honey, rice vinegar, sesame oil, minced garlic, and grated ginger. Set aside.

Heat a tablespoon of cooking oil in a large skillet or wok over medium-high heat. Season the shrimp with salt and pepper, then add them to the hot skillet in a single layer. Cook for 2-3 minutes on each side until they turn pink and opaque. Remove the shrimp from the skillet and set aside.

In the same skillet, add the sesame seeds and toast them for about 1-2 minutes until golden brown and fragrant. Be careful not to burn them.

Return the cooked shrimp to the skillet. Pour the sauce mixture over the shrimp and sesame seeds. Stir well to coat the shrimp evenly with the sauce.

Cook for another 1-2 minutes until the sauce thickens slightly and coats the shrimp.

Remove from heat and transfer the sesame shrimp to a serving dish.

Garnish with sliced green onions.

Serve hot with steamed rice or your favorite side dishes.

Enjoy your delicious sesame shrimp!

Moo Shu Pork

Ingredients:

For the marinade:

- 1 lb (450g) pork tenderloin or pork loin, thinly sliced
- 2 tablespoons soy sauce
- 1 tablespoon rice wine or dry sherry
- 1 teaspoon cornstarch
- 1 teaspoon sesame oil

For the sauce:

- 2 tablespoons hoisin sauce
- 2 tablespoons soy sauce
- 1 tablespoon rice vinegar
- 1 tablespoon honey or brown sugar
- 1 teaspoon sesame oil

For the stir-fry:

- 2 tablespoons vegetable oil
- 3 cloves garlic, minced
- 1 teaspoon ginger, minced
- 1 onion, thinly sliced
- 2 cups shredded cabbage
- 1 cup shredded carrots
- 1 cup sliced mushrooms
- 1 cup sliced bamboo shoots (optional)
- 1 cup sliced wood ear mushrooms (optional)
- 4-6 green onions, thinly sliced
- Salt and pepper to taste
- Mandarin pancakes or flour tortillas, for serving

Instructions:

In a bowl, combine the thinly sliced pork with soy sauce, rice wine or sherry, cornstarch, and sesame oil. Mix well to coat the pork evenly. Let it marinate for at least 20-30 minutes.

In another bowl, mix together hoisin sauce, soy sauce, rice vinegar, honey or brown sugar, and sesame oil to make the sauce. Set aside.

Heat 1 tablespoon of vegetable oil in a large skillet or wok over medium-high heat. Add the marinated pork slices and stir-fry until cooked through, about 3-4 minutes. Remove the pork from the skillet and set aside.

In the same skillet, add another tablespoon of vegetable oil if needed. Add minced garlic and ginger, and stir-fry for about 30 seconds until fragrant.

Add sliced onion, shredded cabbage, shredded carrots, sliced mushrooms, bamboo shoots, and wood ear mushrooms to the skillet. Stir-fry for 3-4 minutes until the vegetables are tender-crisp.

Return the cooked pork to the skillet. Pour the sauce over the pork and vegetables. Stir well to coat everything evenly with the sauce. Cook for an additional 1-2 minutes until heated through.

Season with salt and pepper to taste. Stir in sliced green onions.

Serve the Moo Shu Pork hot with Mandarin pancakes or flour tortillas for wrapping.

To serve, spoon some of the pork and vegetable mixture onto a pancake or tortilla, fold the sides over, and enjoy!

Enjoy your homemade Moo Shu Pork!

Garlic Shrimp Fried Rice

Ingredients:

- 1 lb (450g) shrimp, peeled and deveined
- 3 cups cooked rice (preferably cold, leftover rice works best)
- 4 cloves garlic, minced
- 2 tablespoons vegetable oil
- 2 eggs, lightly beaten
- 1 cup mixed vegetables (such as peas, carrots, corn)
- 2 tablespoons soy sauce
- 1 tablespoon oyster sauce
- 1 teaspoon sesame oil
- Salt and pepper to taste
- Green onions, chopped for garnish (optional)

Instructions:

Heat 1 tablespoon of vegetable oil in a large skillet or wok over medium-high heat. Add the shrimp and cook for 2-3 minutes until they turn pink and opaque. Remove the shrimp from the skillet and set aside.
In the same skillet, add the remaining tablespoon of vegetable oil. Add minced garlic and stir-fry for about 30 seconds until fragrant.
Push the garlic to one side of the skillet and pour the beaten eggs into the empty space. Scramble the eggs until fully cooked, then mix them with the garlic.
Add the mixed vegetables to the skillet and stir-fry for 2-3 minutes until they are tender-crisp.
Add the cooked rice to the skillet, breaking up any clumps with a spatula. Stir-fry the rice with the vegetables and eggs for 3-4 minutes until heated through.
Return the cooked shrimp to the skillet.
Drizzle soy sauce, oyster sauce, and sesame oil over the rice mixture. Stir well to combine and evenly distribute the sauces.
Season with salt and pepper to taste. Stir-fry for another 2-3 minutes until everything is well mixed and heated through.
Remove from heat and garnish with chopped green onions, if desired.
Serve the garlic shrimp fried rice hot as a main dish or side dish.

Enjoy your flavorful garlic shrimp fried rice!

Chicken Lettuce Wraps

Ingredients:

- 1 lb (450g) ground chicken
- 1 tablespoon olive oil
- 2 cloves garlic, minced
- 1 onion, finely chopped
- 1 red bell pepper, finely chopped
- 1 carrot, grated
- 1/4 cup soy sauce
- 2 tablespoons hoisin sauce
- 1 tablespoon rice vinegar
- 1 teaspoon sesame oil
- 1 teaspoon freshly grated ginger
- Salt and pepper, to taste
- Iceberg or butter lettuce leaves, for wrapping
- Optional toppings: chopped green onions, sliced water chestnuts, chopped peanuts, cilantro leaves

Instructions:

Heat olive oil in a large skillet over medium heat. Add minced garlic and cook for about 1 minute until fragrant.
Add chopped onion to the skillet and cook until softened, about 2-3 minutes.
Add ground chicken to the skillet, breaking it up with a spatula, and cook until browned and cooked through, about 5-7 minutes.
Stir in chopped red bell pepper and grated carrot, and cook for another 2-3 minutes until vegetables are slightly softened.
In a small bowl, mix together soy sauce, hoisin sauce, rice vinegar, sesame oil, and freshly grated ginger. Pour the sauce mixture into the skillet with the chicken and vegetables. Stir well to combine.
Season with salt and pepper to taste. Cook for another 2-3 minutes until the sauce is heated through and the flavors are well combined.
To serve, spoon the chicken mixture onto individual lettuce leaves. Top with optional toppings such as chopped green onions, sliced water chestnuts, chopped peanuts, and cilantro leaves.
Roll up the lettuce leaves like a burrito and enjoy!

These chicken lettuce wraps make for a flavorful and satisfying meal or appetizer. Feel free to customize the recipe by adding your favorite vegetables or adjusting the seasonings to suit your taste preferences. Enjoy!

Hunan Chicken

Ingredients:

For the marinade:

- 1 lb (450g) boneless, skinless chicken breast, cut into thin strips
- 2 tablespoons soy sauce
- 1 tablespoon rice wine or dry sherry
- 1 tablespoon cornstarch

For the sauce:

- 2 tablespoons soy sauce
- 2 tablespoons hoisin sauce
- 1 tablespoon rice vinegar
- 1 tablespoon brown sugar
- 2 teaspoons sesame oil
- 1 teaspoon cornstarch

For the stir-fry:

- 2 tablespoons vegetable oil
- 4-5 dried red chili peppers, chopped (adjust to taste)
- 3 cloves garlic, minced
- 1-inch piece of ginger, minced
- 1 onion, thinly sliced
- 1 bell pepper, thinly sliced
- 1 cup broccoli florets
- 1/2 cup sliced mushrooms
- Salt and pepper, to taste
- Cooked rice, for serving

Instructions:

In a bowl, mix together the marinade ingredients: soy sauce, rice wine (or sherry), and cornstarch. Add the chicken strips and toss to coat. Let it marinate for about 15-20 minutes.

In another small bowl, whisk together the sauce ingredients: soy sauce, hoisin sauce, rice vinegar, brown sugar, sesame oil, and cornstarch. Set aside.

Heat vegetable oil in a wok or large skillet over high heat. Add the dried red chili peppers and stir-fry for about 30 seconds until fragrant.
Add minced garlic and ginger to the wok and stir-fry for another 30 seconds.
Add the marinated chicken to the wok and stir-fry until it's cooked through and slightly browned, about 5-6 minutes.
Add sliced onion, bell pepper, broccoli florets, and sliced mushrooms to the wok. Stir-fry for an additional 3-4 minutes until the vegetables are tender-crisp.
Pour the sauce mixture over the chicken and vegetables in the wok. Stir well to coat everything evenly.
Cook for another 2-3 minutes until the sauce thickens and everything is heated through.
Season with salt and pepper to taste.
Serve the Hunan chicken hot over cooked rice.

Enjoy your homemade Hunan chicken with its delicious blend of flavors and spicy kick! Adjust the amount of chili peppers to suit your spice tolerance.

Shrimp with Garlic Sauce

Ingredients:

- 1 lb (450g) large shrimp, peeled and deveined
- 2 tablespoons soy sauce
- 1 tablespoon rice wine or dry sherry
- 1 tablespoon cornstarch
- 2 tablespoons vegetable oil
- 4 cloves garlic, minced
- 1-inch piece of ginger, minced
- 1 onion, thinly sliced
- 1 bell pepper, thinly sliced
- 1 cup sliced mushrooms
- 1/4 cup chicken broth or water
- 2 tablespoons oyster sauce
- 1 tablespoon soy sauce
- 1 teaspoon sugar
- 1 teaspoon sesame oil
- Salt and pepper, to taste
- Green onions, thinly sliced (for garnish)
- Cooked rice, for serving

Instructions:

In a bowl, combine the soy sauce, rice wine (or sherry), and cornstarch. Add the shrimp and toss to coat. Let it marinate for about 15-20 minutes.

Heat vegetable oil in a large skillet or wok over medium-high heat. Add the minced garlic and ginger, and stir-fry for about 30 seconds until fragrant.

Add the marinated shrimp to the skillet and stir-fry until they turn pink and opaque, about 2-3 minutes. Remove the shrimp from the skillet and set aside.

In the same skillet, add a bit more oil if needed. Add the sliced onion, bell pepper, and mushrooms. Stir-fry for about 3-4 minutes until the vegetables are tender-crisp.

In a small bowl, mix together the chicken broth (or water), oyster sauce, soy sauce, sugar, and sesame oil.

Pour the sauce mixture into the skillet with the vegetables. Bring to a simmer and cook for another 2-3 minutes until the sauce slightly thickens.

Return the cooked shrimp to the skillet and toss to coat them evenly with the sauce.
Season with salt and pepper to taste.
Garnish with thinly sliced green onions.
Serve the shrimp with garlic sauce hot over cooked rice.

Enjoy your homemade shrimp with garlic sauce, packed with savory flavors and served with tender shrimp and crisp vegetables! Adjust the seasoning according to your taste preferences.

Beef Chow Fun

Ingredients:

- 12 oz (340g) fresh wide rice noodles (also known as Ho Fun noodles)
- 8 oz (225g) beef flank steak, sliced thinly against the grain
- 2 tablespoons soy sauce
- 1 tablespoon oyster sauce
- 1 tablespoon Shaoxing wine or dry sherry
- 1 teaspoon cornstarch
- 2 tablespoons vegetable oil, divided
- 3 cloves garlic, minced
- 1 onion, thinly sliced
- 1 bell pepper, thinly sliced
- 2 cups bean sprouts
- 2 green onions, chopped (for garnish)
- Salt and pepper, to taste

For the sauce:

- 2 tablespoons soy sauce
- 1 tablespoon oyster sauce
- 1 tablespoon dark soy sauce (for color)
- 1 teaspoon sugar
- 1/2 teaspoon sesame oil

Instructions:

Prepare the rice noodles according to package instructions. If using fresh noodles, they may just need a quick rinse under warm water to separate them.

In a bowl, marinate the sliced beef with soy sauce, oyster sauce, Shaoxing wine (or sherry), and cornstarch. Let it sit for about 15-20 minutes.

In a small bowl, mix together the sauce ingredients: soy sauce, oyster sauce, dark soy sauce, sugar, and sesame oil. Set aside.

Heat 1 tablespoon of vegetable oil in a large skillet or wok over high heat. Add the marinated beef and stir-fry until it's browned and cooked through, about 2-3 minutes. Remove the beef from the skillet and set aside.

In the same skillet, add the remaining tablespoon of vegetable oil. Add minced garlic and stir-fry for about 30 seconds until fragrant.

Add sliced onion and bell pepper to the skillet and stir-fry for about 2-3 minutes until they start to soften.

Add the cooked rice noodles to the skillet, along with the prepared sauce. Toss everything together to coat the noodles evenly.

Add the cooked beef back into the skillet and stir-fry for another 1-2 minutes until everything is heated through.

Add bean sprouts to the skillet and toss everything together for another 1-2 minutes.

Season with salt and pepper to taste.

Garnish with chopped green onions.

Serve hot and enjoy your Beef Chow Fun!

This dish is best enjoyed immediately while the noodles are still tender and the flavors are fresh.

Adjust the seasonings according to your taste preferences.

Five-Spice Pork Ribs

Ingredients:

- 2 lbs (about 900g) pork spare ribs, cut into individual ribs
- 2 tablespoons soy sauce
- 2 tablespoons hoisin sauce
- 1 tablespoon honey or brown sugar
- 2 teaspoons Chinese five-spice powder
- 2 cloves garlic, minced
- 1 tablespoon grated ginger
- 2 tablespoons vegetable oil
- Salt and pepper, to taste
- Chopped green onions and sesame seeds for garnish (optional)

Instructions:

In a bowl, mix together soy sauce, hoisin sauce, honey (or brown sugar), Chinese five-spice powder, minced garlic, and grated ginger to make the marinade.

Place the pork ribs in a shallow dish or large resealable plastic bag. Pour the marinade over the ribs, ensuring they are evenly coated. Marinate the ribs in the refrigerator for at least 2 hours, or preferably overnight, to allow the flavors to develop.

Preheat your oven to 350°F (175°C).

Remove the ribs from the marinade and shake off any excess. Reserve the marinade for later use.

Heat vegetable oil in a large oven-safe skillet or baking dish over medium-high heat. Add the ribs and sear them for about 2-3 minutes on each side until they are browned.

Pour the reserved marinade over the ribs in the skillet.

Cover the skillet or baking dish with aluminum foil and transfer it to the preheated oven.

Bake the ribs for about 1 to 1 1/2 hours, or until the meat is tender and cooked through.

Remove the foil during the last 15 minutes of cooking to allow the ribs to caramelize and develop a nice glaze.

Once the ribs are cooked, remove them from the oven and let them rest for a few minutes.

Garnish with chopped green onions and sesame seeds, if desired.

Serve the five-spice pork ribs hot, and enjoy!

These five-spice pork ribs are delicious served with steamed rice and your favorite vegetables. Adjust the sweetness and spiciness of the marinade to suit your taste preferences.

Honey Walnut Shrimp

Ingredients:

For the shrimp:

- 1 lb (450g) large shrimp, peeled and deveined
- Salt and pepper, to taste
- 1/2 cup cornstarch
- Vegetable oil, for frying

For the sauce:

- 1/2 cup mayonnaise
- 3 tablespoons honey
- 1 tablespoon condensed milk
- 1 tablespoon lemon juice

For the candied walnuts:

- 1/2 cup walnut halves
- 1/4 cup granulated sugar
- 1 tablespoon water

Instructions:

Season the shrimp with salt and pepper.
Dredge the shrimp in cornstarch, shaking off any excess.
Heat vegetable oil in a deep skillet or wok over medium-high heat. Fry the shrimp in batches until they are golden and crispy, about 2-3 minutes per side. Transfer the cooked shrimp to a paper towel-lined plate to drain excess oil.
To make the sauce, whisk together mayonnaise, honey, condensed milk, and lemon juice in a bowl until smooth. Adjust sweetness or tartness to taste by adding more honey or lemon juice if desired.
For the candied walnuts, place walnut halves in a dry skillet over medium heat. Toast them for a few minutes, stirring constantly, until they are fragrant. Remove the walnuts from the skillet and set aside.
In the same skillet, combine granulated sugar and water. Cook over medium heat, stirring constantly, until the sugar dissolves and the mixture starts to bubble. Add the toasted walnuts to the skillet and stir to coat them evenly with the sugar

syrup. Continue cooking and stirring until the sugar crystallizes and coats the walnuts, forming a crunchy coating. Remove the candied walnuts from the skillet and let them cool on parchment paper.

Once the candied walnuts are cooled, chop them into smaller pieces if desired.

In a large bowl, toss the fried shrimp with the honey sauce until they are evenly coated.

Gently fold in the chopped candied walnuts until they are distributed throughout the shrimp.

Serve the honey walnut shrimp hot, garnished with additional chopped walnuts or sliced green onions if desired.

Enjoy your homemade honey walnut shrimp, a delightful combination of crispy shrimp, creamy sauce, and crunchy candied walnuts!

Veggie Lo Mein

Ingredients:

- 8 oz (about 225g) lo mein noodles or spaghetti
- 2 tablespoons vegetable oil
- 2 cloves garlic, minced
- 1-inch piece of ginger, minced
- 1 onion, thinly sliced
- 1 bell pepper, thinly sliced
- 1 carrot, julienned or thinly sliced
- 1 cup sliced mushrooms
- 2 cups shredded cabbage or bok choy
- 1/2 cup snow peas, trimmed
- 2 tablespoons soy sauce
- 1 tablespoon oyster sauce (optional)
- 1 tablespoon hoisin sauce (optional)
- 1 teaspoon sesame oil
- Salt and pepper, to taste
- Chopped green onions, for garnish (optional)
- Sesame seeds, for garnish (optional)

Instructions:

Cook the lo mein noodles according to the package instructions until they are al dente. Drain and rinse with cold water to stop the cooking process. Set aside.
Heat vegetable oil in a large skillet or wok over medium-high heat. Add minced garlic and ginger, and stir-fry for about 30 seconds until fragrant.
Add sliced onion, bell pepper, carrot, and mushrooms to the skillet. Stir-fry for about 2-3 minutes until the vegetables start to soften.
Add shredded cabbage or bok choy and snow peas to the skillet. Stir-fry for another 2-3 minutes until all the vegetables are tender-crisp.
In a small bowl, mix together soy sauce, oyster sauce (if using), hoisin sauce (if using), and sesame oil.
Add the cooked lo mein noodles to the skillet with the vegetables.
Pour the sauce mixture over the noodles and vegetables. Toss everything together until the noodles and vegetables are evenly coated with the sauce.
Season with salt and pepper to taste.

Continue to cook for another 2-3 minutes until everything is heated through.
Garnish with chopped green onions and sesame seeds, if desired.
Serve the Veggie Lo Mein hot as a main dish or side dish.

Enjoy your homemade Veggie Lo Mein, packed with colorful vegetables and delicious flavors! Feel free to customize the recipe by adding your favorite vegetables or adjusting the seasonings to suit your taste preferences.

Lemon Garlic Broccoli

Ingredients:

- 1 head of broccoli, cut into florets
- 2 cloves of garlic, minced
- 1 lemon, zest and juice
- 2 tablespoons olive oil
- Salt and pepper to taste

Instructions:

Start by washing the broccoli under cold water and then cutting it into bite-sized florets. Set aside.

Heat the olive oil in a large skillet over medium heat. Once the oil is hot, add the minced garlic to the skillet and sauté for about 1 minute, or until fragrant.

Add the broccoli florets to the skillet and toss them to coat them evenly with the garlic-infused oil. Allow the broccoli to cook for about 5-7 minutes, stirring occasionally, until it becomes tender but still crisp.

While the broccoli is cooking, zest the lemon and then cut it in half. Squeeze the juice from one half of the lemon over the broccoli in the skillet.

Once the broccoli is cooked to your desired level of tenderness, remove the skillet from the heat. Sprinkle the lemon zest over the broccoli and toss everything together to combine.

Taste the broccoli and adjust the seasoning with salt and pepper as needed.

Transfer the lemon garlic broccoli to a serving dish and serve hot as a delicious and nutritious side dish.

Feel free to adjust the quantities of lemon, garlic, or any other seasonings according to your personal preference. Enjoy your lemon garlic broccoli!

Pineapple Chicken

Ingredients:

- 1 lb (450g) boneless, skinless chicken breast or thighs, cut into bite-sized pieces
- 2 cups fresh pineapple chunks (or canned pineapple chunks, drained)
- 1 red bell pepper, diced
- 1 onion, diced
- 3 cloves garlic, minced
- 1 tablespoon ginger, minced
- 1/4 cup soy sauce
- 1/4 cup pineapple juice (reserved from the pineapple chunks if using canned)
- 2 tablespoons honey or brown sugar
- 1 tablespoon rice vinegar
- 1 tablespoon cornstarch
- 2 tablespoons vegetable oil
- Salt and pepper to taste
- Optional: chopped green onions and sesame seeds for garnish

Instructions:

In a small bowl, whisk together soy sauce, pineapple juice, honey (or brown sugar), rice vinegar, and cornstarch. Set aside.

Heat vegetable oil in a large skillet or wok over medium-high heat. Add diced chicken pieces to the skillet and season with salt and pepper. Cook until the chicken is browned and cooked through, about 5-6 minutes. Remove the chicken from the skillet and set aside.

In the same skillet, add a bit more oil if needed. Add diced onion, minced garlic, and minced ginger. Sauté until fragrant and onions are softened, about 2-3 minutes.

Add diced red bell pepper to the skillet and cook for an additional 2-3 minutes until it starts to soften.

Return the cooked chicken to the skillet. Pour the prepared sauce over the chicken and vegetables. Stir well to combine.

Add pineapple chunks to the skillet and gently stir to distribute them evenly. Allow the mixture to simmer for 2-3 minutes, or until the sauce thickens and coats the chicken and pineapple.

Taste and adjust seasoning if necessary.

Once the sauce has thickened and the chicken is heated through, remove the skillet from the heat.
Garnish with chopped green onions and sesame seeds if desired.
Serve the pineapple chicken hot over steamed rice or noodles.

Enjoy your delicious pineapple chicken!

Crispy Tofu with Chili Sauce

Ingredients:

For the crispy tofu:

- 1 block (about 14 oz or 400g) firm tofu, pressed and cut into cubes
- 1/4 cup cornstarch or cornflour
- 2 tablespoons soy sauce
- 1 tablespoon rice vinegar
- 1 teaspoon sesame oil
- Vegetable oil, for frying

For the chili sauce:

- 2 tablespoons soy sauce
- 2 tablespoons rice vinegar
- 2 tablespoons water
- 2 tablespoons sweet chili sauce
- 1 tablespoon honey or maple syrup
- 1 tablespoon Sriracha sauce (adjust to taste for desired spiciness)
- 2 cloves garlic, minced
- 1 teaspoon grated ginger
- 1 teaspoon cornstarch dissolved in 1 tablespoon water (optional, for thickening)

For garnish:

- Toasted sesame seeds
- Sliced green onions

Instructions:

Press the tofu: Wrap the block of tofu in paper towels and place it on a plate. Put a heavy object on top, like a cast-iron skillet or a few cans, and let it sit for about 30 minutes to press out excess moisture. This helps the tofu get crispier when fried.

Prepare the crispy tofu: In a shallow bowl, mix together the cornstarch, soy sauce, rice vinegar, and sesame oil. Toss the tofu cubes in the mixture until they're evenly coated.

Heat vegetable oil in a large skillet or frying pan over medium-high heat. Once the oil is hot, carefully add the tofu cubes in a single layer, making sure not to overcrowd the pan. Fry the tofu until golden and crispy on all sides, about 2-3 minutes per side. Remove the tofu from the pan and place it on a plate lined with paper towels to drain excess oil.

Prepare the chili sauce: In a small saucepan, combine soy sauce, rice vinegar, water, sweet chili sauce, honey or maple syrup, Sriracha sauce, minced garlic, and grated ginger. Bring the mixture to a simmer over medium heat, stirring occasionally.

Optional: If you prefer a thicker sauce, add the cornstarch mixture to the saucepan and stir until the sauce thickens slightly.

Once the sauce reaches your desired consistency, remove it from the heat.

Toss the crispy tofu cubes in the chili sauce until they're evenly coated.

Serve the crispy tofu with chili sauce hot, garnished with toasted sesame seeds and sliced green onions.

Enjoy your delicious crispy tofu with chili sauce as a flavorful appetizer or main dish!

Vegetable Chow Fun

Ingredients:

- 8 oz (225g) wide rice noodles (Chow Fun noodles)
- 2 tablespoons vegetable oil
- 2 cloves garlic, minced
- 1 inch piece of ginger, minced
- 1 onion, thinly sliced
- 1 red bell pepper, thinly sliced
- 1 carrot, julienned
- 2 cups bean sprouts
- 2 scallions (green onions), chopped
- Salt and pepper to taste

For the sauce:

- 3 tablespoons soy sauce
- 2 tablespoons oyster sauce (optional for non-vegetarian version)
- 1 tablespoon sesame oil
- 1 tablespoon rice vinegar
- 1 teaspoon sugar
- 1/2 teaspoon white pepper

Instructions:

Cook the rice noodles according to the package instructions. Once cooked, drain and rinse the noodles under cold water to stop the cooking process. Set aside.
In a small bowl, whisk together all the sauce ingredients: soy sauce, oyster sauce (if using), sesame oil, rice vinegar, sugar, and white pepper. Set aside.
Heat vegetable oil in a large skillet or wok over medium-high heat. Add minced garlic and ginger, and stir-fry for about 30 seconds until fragrant.
Add sliced onions, red bell peppers, and julienned carrots to the skillet. Stir-fry for 2-3 minutes until the vegetables are slightly softened but still crisp.
Add the cooked rice noodles to the skillet, tossing them with the vegetables.
Pour the sauce over the noodles and vegetables. Toss everything together until well combined and heated through.

Add bean sprouts and chopped scallions to the skillet, tossing them with the noodles and vegetables for another 1-2 minutes until the bean sprouts are slightly wilted.
Taste and adjust seasoning with salt and pepper if needed.
Once everything is heated through and well combined, remove the skillet from the heat.
Serve vegetable chow fun hot as a delicious and satisfying main dish.

Enjoy your homemade vegetable chow fun! You can customize this dish by adding other vegetables such as mushrooms, snow peas, or baby corn if desired.

Sweet and Sour Tofu

Ingredients:

For the tofu:

- 1 block (about 14 oz or 400g) firm tofu, cut into cubes
- 1/4 cup cornstarch or cornflour
- Vegetable oil, for frying
- Salt and pepper, to taste

For the sweet and sour sauce:

- 1/4 cup ketchup
- 3 tablespoons rice vinegar
- 2 tablespoons soy sauce
- 2 tablespoons honey or brown sugar
- 1 tablespoon cornstarch
- 1/4 cup water
- 1 tablespoon vegetable oil
- 1 bell pepper, diced
- 1 onion, diced
- 1 cup pineapple chunks (fresh or canned), drained

Instructions:

Press the tofu: Wrap the tofu block in paper towels and place it on a plate. Put a heavy object on top, like a cast-iron skillet or a few cans, and let it sit for about 30 minutes to press out excess moisture. This helps the tofu get firmer and crispier when fried.

Once pressed, cut the tofu into cubes and season with salt and pepper.

Coat the tofu cubes with cornstarch or cornflour, shaking off any excess.

Heat vegetable oil in a large skillet or frying pan over medium-high heat. Once the oil is hot, add the tofu cubes in a single layer. Fry until golden and crispy on all sides, about 3-4 minutes per side. Remove the tofu from the pan and place it on a plate lined with paper towels to drain excess oil.

In a small bowl, whisk together the ketchup, rice vinegar, soy sauce, honey or brown sugar, cornstarch, and water to make the sweet and sour sauce. Set aside.

In the same skillet, heat 1 tablespoon of vegetable oil over medium heat. Add diced bell pepper and onion, and sauté until they start to soften, about 2-3 minutes.

Add the pineapple chunks to the skillet and cook for another 1-2 minutes.

Pour the sweet and sour sauce into the skillet with the vegetables and pineapple. Stir well to combine.

Bring the sauce to a simmer and cook for 2-3 minutes, stirring constantly, until it thickens.

Once the sauce has thickened, add the fried tofu cubes to the skillet. Gently toss everything together until the tofu is coated with the sweet and sour sauce.

Serve the sweet and sour tofu hot over steamed rice or noodles.

Enjoy your delicious sweet and sour tofu! You can garnish it with sesame seeds and chopped green onions for extra flavor and presentation if desired.

Spicy Szechuan Shrimp

Ingredients:

- 1 lb (450g) large shrimp, peeled and deveined
- 2 tablespoons vegetable oil
- 3 cloves garlic, minced
- 1-inch piece of ginger, minced
- 2-3 dried red chilies (adjust to taste), chopped
- 1 bell pepper, thinly sliced
- 1/2 cup chopped green onions
- 1/4 cup peanuts or cashews (optional, for garnish)
- Salt and pepper to taste

For the marinade:

- 2 tablespoons soy sauce
- 1 tablespoon rice vinegar
- 1 tablespoon cornstarch

For the sauce:

- 2 tablespoons soy sauce
- 1 tablespoon hoisin sauce
- 1 tablespoon rice vinegar
- 1 tablespoon honey or brown sugar
- 1 teaspoon sesame oil
- 1 teaspoon Szechuan peppercorns, crushed
- 1 teaspoon chili paste or chili sauce (adjust to taste)
- 1/4 cup chicken broth or water
- 1 tablespoon cornstarch

Instructions:

In a bowl, combine the shrimp with the marinade ingredients: soy sauce, rice vinegar, and cornstarch. Mix well to coat the shrimp evenly. Let it marinate for about 15-20 minutes.

In another bowl, whisk together all the sauce ingredients: soy sauce, hoisin sauce, rice vinegar, honey or brown sugar, sesame oil, crushed Szechuan peppercorns, chili paste or chili sauce, chicken broth or water, and cornstarch. Set aside.

Heat vegetable oil in a large skillet or wok over medium-high heat. Add minced garlic, minced ginger, and chopped dried red chilies. Stir-fry for about 30 seconds until fragrant.

Add the marinated shrimp to the skillet. Stir-fry for 2-3 minutes until the shrimp start to turn pink and are almost cooked through. Remove the shrimp from the skillet and set aside.

In the same skillet, add the sliced bell pepper and chopped green onions. Stir-fry for 2-3 minutes until the vegetables are slightly softened.

Return the cooked shrimp to the skillet. Pour the prepared sauce over the shrimp and vegetables.

Stir well to coat everything evenly in the sauce. Cook for another 2-3 minutes, stirring occasionally, until the sauce thickens and the shrimp are fully cooked.

Optional: Garnish the spicy Szechuan shrimp with chopped peanuts or cashews for added crunch and flavor.

Serve hot over steamed rice or noodles.

Enjoy your delicious and spicy Szechuan shrimp! Adjust the amount of chili paste or chili sauce according to your preferred level of spiciness.

Hot and Sour Soup

Ingredients:

- 6 cups chicken or vegetable broth
- 8 oz (225g) firm tofu, cut into small cubes
- 4 oz (115g) mushrooms (such as shiitake or button), thinly sliced
- 1/2 cup bamboo shoots, thinly sliced
- 1/4 cup rice vinegar
- 3 tablespoons soy sauce
- 1 tablespoon sesame oil
- 1 tablespoon chili paste or chili sauce (adjust to taste)
- 1 tablespoon cornstarch, dissolved in 2 tablespoons water
- 2 eggs, lightly beaten
- 1/4 cup sliced green onions
- Salt and pepper to taste
- Optional: 1 teaspoon grated ginger, 1 clove minced garlic, 1 teaspoon sugar

Instructions:

In a large pot, bring the chicken or vegetable broth to a simmer over medium heat.

Add the tofu cubes, sliced mushrooms, and bamboo shoots to the simmering broth. If you're using grated ginger and minced garlic for extra flavor, add them to the pot now.

In a small bowl, mix together the rice vinegar, soy sauce, sesame oil, and chili paste or chili sauce. Adjust the amount of chili paste according to your desired level of spiciness. If you prefer a sweeter soup, you can also add a teaspoon of sugar to the mixture.

Pour the vinegar and soy sauce mixture into the pot of simmering broth and stir well. Let the soup simmer for about 5 minutes to allow the flavors to meld together.

Slowly pour the beaten eggs into the soup while stirring gently with a fork or chopsticks. The eggs will form thin ribbons in the soup.

In a small bowl, dissolve the cornstarch in water to create a slurry. Slowly pour the cornstarch slurry into the soup while stirring constantly. This will help thicken the soup slightly.

Continue to simmer the soup for another 2-3 minutes until it reaches your desired consistency. If the soup is too thick, you can add a little more broth or water to thin it out.

Taste the soup and adjust the seasoning with salt and pepper if needed.

Stir in the sliced green onions just before serving.

Ladle the hot and sour soup into bowls and serve immediately.

Enjoy your delicious and comforting hot and sour soup! It's perfect for warming up on a chilly day or as a starter for a Chinese-inspired meal.

Chicken and Cashew Nuts

Ingredients:

- 500g boneless, skinless chicken breast, cut into bite-sized pieces
- 1 cup raw cashew nuts
- 1 red bell pepper, sliced
- 1 green bell pepper, sliced
- 1 onion, sliced
- 3 cloves garlic, minced
- 2 tablespoons soy sauce
- 1 tablespoon oyster sauce
- 1 tablespoon hoisin sauce
- 1 tablespoon sesame oil
- 1 teaspoon cornstarch
- 1 teaspoon sugar
- Salt and pepper to taste
- Vegetable oil for cooking
- Spring onions, chopped for garnish (optional)
- Cooked rice for serving

Instructions:

In a small bowl, mix together soy sauce, oyster sauce, hoisin sauce, sesame oil, cornstarch, and sugar. Set aside.

Heat some vegetable oil in a large skillet or wok over medium-high heat.

Add the minced garlic and stir-fry for about 30 seconds until fragrant.

Add the chicken pieces to the skillet and cook until they are browned and cooked through, about 5-7 minutes.

Remove the chicken from the skillet and set aside.

In the same skillet, add a bit more oil if needed, and then add the sliced onions and bell peppers. Stir-fry for about 2-3 minutes until they are slightly softened but still crisp.

Add the cashew nuts to the skillet and continue to stir-fry for another 1-2 minutes until they are lightly toasted.

Return the cooked chicken to the skillet and pour the sauce mixture over the chicken and vegetables. Stir well to combine.

Cook for another 2-3 minutes, stirring occasionally, until the sauce has thickened slightly and everything is heated through.
Season with salt and pepper to taste.
Garnish with chopped spring onions if desired.
Serve the Chicken and Cashew Nuts hot over cooked rice.

Enjoy your delicious Chicken and Cashew Nuts!

General Tso's Cauliflower

Ingredients:

For the cauliflower:

- 1 large head of cauliflower, cut into florets
- 1 cup all-purpose flour
- 1 cup water
- 1 teaspoon garlic powder
- 1 teaspoon onion powder
- Salt and pepper, to taste
- Vegetable oil, for frying

For the sauce:

- 1/4 cup soy sauce
- 2 tablespoons hoisin sauce
- 2 tablespoons rice vinegar
- 2 tablespoons honey or maple syrup
- 1 tablespoon cornstarch
- 1 teaspoon sesame oil
- 2 cloves garlic, minced
- 1 teaspoon grated ginger
- 1/4 teaspoon red pepper flakes (adjust to taste)
- Sesame seeds, for garnish (optional)
- Sliced green onions, for garnish (optional)

Instructions:

In a large bowl, whisk together the all-purpose flour, water, garlic powder, onion powder, salt, and pepper to make a batter. The consistency should be similar to pancake batter.
Heat vegetable oil in a large skillet or pot over medium-high heat for frying.
Dip each cauliflower floret into the batter, shaking off any excess, and carefully place it into the hot oil. Fry in batches until golden brown and crispy, about 4-5 minutes per batch. Remove the fried cauliflower florets and place them on a paper towel-lined plate to drain any excess oil.

In a separate mixing bowl, whisk together soy sauce, hoisin sauce, rice vinegar, honey or maple syrup, cornstarch, sesame oil, minced garlic, grated ginger, and red pepper flakes until well combined.

Once all the cauliflower florets are fried, discard any excess oil from the skillet, leaving about 1 tablespoon.

Add the sauce mixture to the skillet and cook over medium heat, stirring constantly, until the sauce thickens and becomes glossy, about 2-3 minutes.

Add the fried cauliflower florets to the skillet and toss until they are evenly coated in the sauce.

Cook for another 2-3 minutes, stirring occasionally, to heat the cauliflower through and allow the flavors to meld.

Remove from heat and transfer the General Tso's Cauliflower to a serving dish. Garnish with sesame seeds and sliced green onions, if desired.

Serve hot over steamed rice or noodles.

Enjoy your General Tso's Cauliflower!

Shrimp and Lobster Sauce

Ingredients:

- 1 lb (450g) large shrimp, peeled and deveined
- 2 tablespoons vegetable oil
- 3 cloves garlic, minced
- 1 tablespoon ginger, minced
- 1/4 cup fermented black beans, rinsed and mashed
- 1 cup chicken or vegetable broth
- 2 tablespoons soy sauce
- 1 tablespoon oyster sauce
- 1 tablespoon Shaoxing wine (or dry sherry)
- 1 teaspoon sugar
- 2 tablespoons cornstarch mixed with 2 tablespoons water (cornstarch slurry)
- 2 large eggs, lightly beaten
- 1 cup frozen peas, thawed (optional)
- Salt and pepper to taste
- Cooked rice for serving
- Chopped green onions for garnish (optional)

Instructions:

Heat vegetable oil in a large skillet or wok over medium-high heat.
Add minced garlic and ginger to the skillet and stir-fry for about 30 seconds until fragrant.
Add the mashed fermented black beans to the skillet and stir-fry for another 1-2 minutes.
Add the shrimp to the skillet and cook until they turn pink and opaque, about 2-3 minutes. Remove the shrimp from the skillet and set aside.
In the same skillet, add chicken or vegetable broth, soy sauce, oyster sauce, Shaoxing wine, and sugar. Stir to combine and bring the mixture to a simmer.
Once the sauce is simmering, gradually pour in the cornstarch slurry while stirring continuously until the sauce thickens to your desired consistency.
Slowly pour the beaten eggs into the simmering sauce while stirring gently with a spoon to create ribbons of egg throughout the sauce.
Add the cooked shrimp back to the skillet along with the thawed peas (if using). Stir gently to combine and heat through.

Season with salt and pepper to taste.
Serve the Shrimp and Lobster Sauce hot over cooked rice.
Garnish with chopped green onions if desired.

Enjoy your delicious homemade Shrimp and Lobster Sauce!

Beef with Oyster Sauce

Ingredients:

- 1 lb (450g) beef steak (such as flank steak or sirloin), thinly sliced against the grain
- 2 tablespoons vegetable oil
- 3 cloves garlic, minced
- 1 tablespoon ginger, minced
- 1 onion, thinly sliced
- 1 bell pepper, thinly sliced
- 1/2 cup sliced mushrooms (optional)
- 1/4 cup oyster sauce
- 2 tablespoons soy sauce
- 1 tablespoon hoisin sauce
- 1 tablespoon Shaoxing wine (or dry sherry)
- 1 teaspoon sugar
- 1 teaspoon cornstarch mixed with 2 teaspoons water (cornstarch slurry)
- Salt and pepper to taste
- Cooked rice or noodles for serving
- Chopped green onions for garnish (optional)
- Sesame seeds for garnish (optional)

Instructions:

Heat vegetable oil in a large skillet or wok over medium-high heat.
Add minced garlic and ginger to the skillet and stir-fry for about 30 seconds until fragrant.
Add the thinly sliced beef to the skillet and stir-fry until it's browned and cooked to your desired doneness. Remove the beef from the skillet and set aside.
In the same skillet, add a bit more oil if needed, and then add the sliced onion, bell pepper, and mushrooms (if using). Stir-fry for about 2-3 minutes until the vegetables are slightly softened but still crisp.
Return the cooked beef to the skillet with the vegetables.
In a small bowl, mix together oyster sauce, soy sauce, hoisin sauce, Shaoxing wine, sugar, and the cornstarch slurry.
Pour the sauce mixture over the beef and vegetables in the skillet. Stir well to coat everything evenly.

Cook for another 2-3 minutes, stirring occasionally, until the sauce has thickened and everything is heated through.
Season with salt and pepper to taste.
Serve the Beef with Oyster Sauce hot over cooked rice or noodles.
Garnish with chopped green onions and sesame seeds if desired.

Enjoy your delicious Beef with Oyster Sauce!

Veggie Spring Roll Bowls

Ingredients:

For the bowl:

- 8 ounces (225g) rice noodles or vermicelli noodles
- 1 tablespoon sesame oil
- 2 cups shredded cabbage
- 1 large carrot, julienned or grated
- 1 red bell pepper, thinly sliced
- 1 cucumber, julienned or thinly sliced
- 1 cup bean sprouts
- 1/4 cup chopped fresh cilantro or mint leaves
- 1/4 cup chopped roasted peanuts (optional)
- Lime wedges for serving (optional)

For the protein (choose one):

- 1 block (14-16 ounces) extra-firm tofu, pressed and cubed OR
- 1 lb (450g) cooked shrimp, peeled and deveined OR
- 1 lb (450g) cooked chicken breast, shredded OR
- 1 lb (450g) cooked beef or pork, thinly sliced

For the sauce:

- 1/4 cup soy sauce
- 2 tablespoons rice vinegar
- 1 tablespoon sesame oil
- 1 tablespoon honey or maple syrup
- 1 clove garlic, minced
- 1 teaspoon grated ginger
- 1 teaspoon sriracha or chili sauce (optional, for heat)
- 1 tablespoon water (optional, to adjust consistency)

Instructions:

Cook the rice noodles according to the package instructions. Once cooked, drain and rinse under cold water to stop the cooking process. Toss the noodles with 1 tablespoon of sesame oil to prevent sticking and set aside.

Prepare the protein of your choice (tofu, shrimp, chicken, beef, or pork) according to your preference. If using tofu, you can pan-fry or bake it until golden brown and crispy.

In a small bowl, whisk together the soy sauce, rice vinegar, sesame oil, honey or maple syrup, minced garlic, grated ginger, and sriracha (if using). If the sauce is too thick, you can thin it out with a tablespoon of water.

In large serving bowls, divide the cooked rice noodles evenly among them.

Arrange the shredded cabbage, julienned carrot, sliced bell pepper, julienned cucumber, bean sprouts, and protein of your choice (tofu, shrimp, chicken, beef, or pork) on top of the noodles.

Drizzle the prepared sauce over the bowls.

Garnish each bowl with chopped fresh cilantro or mint leaves and chopped roasted peanuts (if using).

Serve the Veggie Spring Roll Bowls immediately with lime wedges on the side for squeezing over the top, if desired.

Enjoy your delicious and nutritious Veggie Spring Roll Bowls!

Feel free to customize the ingredients and protein according to your preferences and dietary restrictions.

Sesame Ginger Bok Choy

Ingredients:

- 4-6 baby bok choy heads, washed and halved lengthwise
- 2 tablespoons sesame oil
- 2 cloves garlic, minced
- 1 tablespoon fresh ginger, minced
- 2 tablespoons soy sauce
- 1 tablespoon rice vinegar
- 1 tablespoon honey or maple syrup
- 1 teaspoon cornstarch
- 2 tablespoons water
- Sesame seeds for garnish
- Optional: red pepper flakes for added heat
- Optional: sliced green onions for garnish

Instructions:

In a small bowl, mix together soy sauce, rice vinegar, honey or maple syrup, cornstarch, and water to make the sauce. Set aside.
Heat sesame oil in a large skillet or wok over medium-high heat.
Add minced garlic and ginger to the skillet and stir-fry for about 30 seconds until fragrant.
Add the bok choy halves to the skillet, cut side down. Cook for about 2-3 minutes until they start to brown slightly.
Flip the bok choy halves over and continue to cook for another 2-3 minutes until they are tender-crisp.
Pour the prepared sauce over the bok choy in the skillet. Stir gently to coat the bok choy evenly with the sauce.
Cook for another 1-2 minutes, allowing the sauce to thicken slightly.
If using red pepper flakes for added heat, sprinkle them over the bok choy and stir to combine.
Remove the skillet from heat and transfer the Sesame Ginger Bok Choy to a serving dish.
Garnish with sesame seeds and sliced green onions if desired.
Serve hot as a side dish or over steamed rice as a main dish.

Enjoy your flavorful Sesame Ginger Bok Choy!

Crispy Orange Tofu

Ingredients:

For the tofu:

- 1 block (about 14 oz) extra-firm tofu, pressed and drained
- 1/2 cup cornstarch or arrowroot powder
- 2-3 tablespoons vegetable oil, for frying
- Salt and pepper, to taste

For the orange sauce:

- 1/2 cup orange juice
- Zest of 1 orange
- 3 tablespoons soy sauce or tamari
- 2 tablespoons rice vinegar
- 2 tablespoons maple syrup or brown sugar
- 2 cloves garlic, minced
- 1 teaspoon grated ginger
- 1 tablespoon cornstarch or arrowroot powder mixed with 2 tablespoons water (to thicken)

Optional garnish:

- Sliced green onions
- Sesame seeds
- Red pepper flakes

Instructions:

Press the tofu: Wrap the block of tofu in a clean kitchen towel or paper towels. Place a heavy object on top (like a cast-iron skillet or books) and let it sit for about 20-30 minutes to remove excess moisture.

Prepare the tofu: Once pressed, slice the tofu into cubes or rectangles, depending on your preference. Season with salt and pepper, then coat each piece in cornstarch or arrowroot powder, shaking off any excess.

Fry the tofu: Heat the vegetable oil in a large skillet over medium-high heat. Once hot, add the tofu pieces in a single layer, making sure not to overcrowd the pan. Fry until golden brown and crispy on all sides, about 3-4 minutes per side. Transfer the cooked tofu to a plate lined with paper towels to drain any excess oil.

Make the orange sauce: In a small saucepan, combine the orange juice, orange zest, soy sauce, rice vinegar, maple syrup or brown sugar, minced garlic, and grated ginger. Bring to a simmer over medium heat.

Thicken the sauce: In a small bowl, mix the cornstarch or arrowroot powder with water until smooth. Stir the mixture into the simmering sauce and cook for another 1-2 minutes, or until the sauce has thickened to your desired consistency.

Combine tofu and sauce: Once the sauce has thickened, add the fried tofu to the saucepan and gently toss to coat each piece evenly with the orange sauce.

Serve: Transfer the crispy orange tofu to a serving dish and garnish with sliced green onions, sesame seeds, and red pepper flakes if desired. Serve hot with steamed rice or your favorite veggies.

Enjoy your delicious crispy orange tofu!

www.ingramcontent.com/pod-product-compliance
Lightning Source LLC
LaVergne TN
LVHW081607060526
838201LV00054B/2120